# EISAH AND THE STRING

## By
## A'la Eisah & Medinah Eatman

*JOURNAL JOY*

*An Imprint of Journal Joy Publishers*

*www.thejournaljoy.com*

For information on publishing, contact Journal Joy at Info@thejournaljoy.com.

www.thejournaljoy.com

**Summary**: Eisah absolutely adores his string. He takes his string everywhere; he loves to play with it in all kinds of fun ways! Eisah was having a blast with his string, as always, until......oh, no! Something devastating happened today. Eisah lost his string!

Follow Eisah on his quest to find his beloved string with the wisdom and love of his family guiding the way in Eisah and the String.

**Paperback ISBN:**  978-1-957751-11-5

**Ebook ISBN:**     978-1-957751-12-2

**Edited** by: Riel Felice

First paperback edition, 2022

I like to play with my string.

I like to wrap my string around the chair.

My auntie—she's an engineer—said a pulley is a simple machine that helps us lift heavy things.

I like to lay my string on the floor and make it look like a sound wave.

My grandpa—he's a doctor—told me that sound waves vibrate. The waves travel into our inner ear, and then go to our brain, so we can hear things.

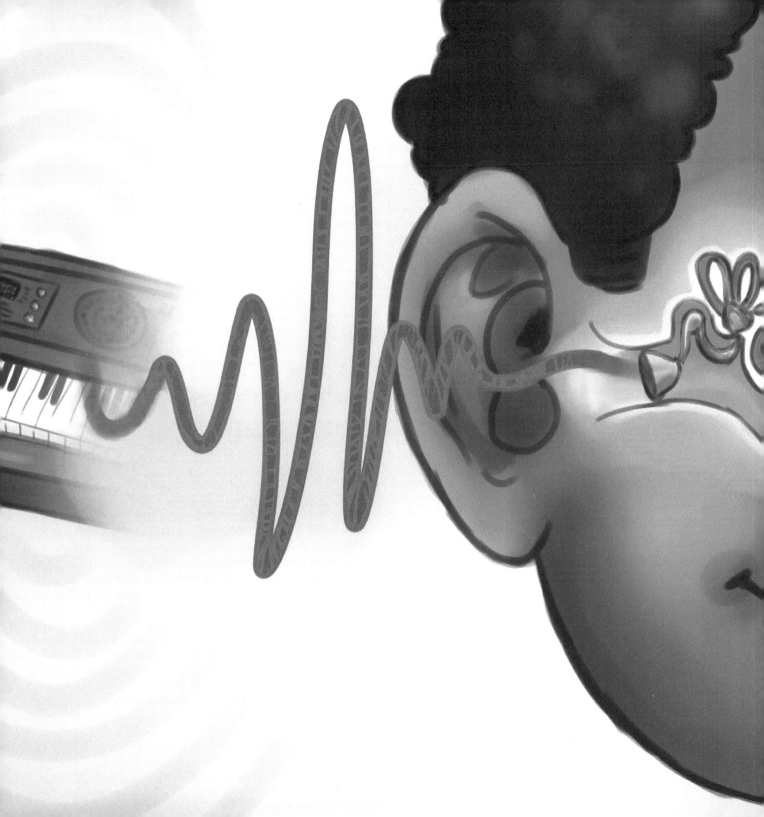

Sometimes, I beg my mom to help me build a zipline with my string.

All you need is a string, a cup, a spool, and a pipe cleaner! It's so fun!

My mom, the ScienceTeacherMom, said that ziplines move with the help of gravity, and they go really fast!

I can pretend that it's a jump rope, a fishing pole, or a belt like Daddy.

Today, I lost my string.

I was so sad. I started to cry.

"Let's go find it," says my little brother, Bilal.

We looked everywhere!

We looked in the toy box—we did not find it.

We looked in the closet—we did not find it!

I was so frustrated. I wanted to quit. My dad came into the room and said, "Do we have a problem? And I responded slowly, with my head still down, "No." "What do we have?" he questioned. I recited, "We have an opportunity." I puffed up my shoulders and tilted my head up to my dad. He put his strong hand on my shoulders and told me to relax and think about where the string might be.

I took a deep breath. I put my finger on my head, and I thought and thought.

Then, I remembered where I put it—it was in my room under my pillow. Sometimes, I like to sleep with it!

I ran to get it. I'm so happy!

"Good night, String!"

# STEM ZIPLINE

## MATERIALS

bobbin

pipe cleaners

string

paper cup

any other household materials that you would like to experiment with

1. Decorate the cup however you choose.

2. Poke holes into the side of the cup. Then thread a pipe cleaner through the hole to create a handle.

3. Take another pipe cleaner and form a hook. Then thread the bobbin on the hook.

4. Tie each end of the string to something sturdy, such as a chair or a door knob. Make sure that it is diagonal.

5. Experiment with using the basket on the zip line string! How does adding extra weight affect the zip line basket?

# ABOUT THE AUTHORS:

# A'la Eisah Eatman

A'la Eisah is a 5-year-old scholar who loves to read, do math problems, explore science concepts, complete puzzles, and do basic coding on his tablet. He learned to read by the time he was 2 years old and currently enjoys reading small chapter books. He can find joy in simple everyday things, like a piece of string, and connect it to things he has already learned.

# Medinah Eatman

Medinah Eatman was born in New York but currently lives in Northern New Jersey with her husband and children. If she's not doing science activities with her sons, you can find her traveling the world, indulging in a good book or hanging out with her family! In 2020, she became fondly known as the Science.Teacher.Mom for helping homeschooling parents and teachers engage their learners by delivering engaging STEM kits! She enjoys sharing fun, hands-on science activities and experiments with children of all ages. Medinah's passion is to guide the minds of these young scientists in each classroom by showing them that science can be fun, accessible, and interesting!

CPSIA information can be obtained
at www.ICGtesting.com
Printed in the USA
BVHW020401241022
650102BV00023B/9